C0-AVD-680

TELEVISION WORKS LIKE THIS

THIRD REVISED EDITION

JEANNE AND ROBERT BENDICK

WHITTLESEY HOUSE · McGRAW-HILL

NEW YORK · TORONTO · LONDON

THANK
YOU

To all the television people
on two coasts who helped
with this book.

3d Edition
TELEVISION WORKS LIKE THIS
Copyright © 1959 by the McGraw-Hill Book Company, Inc. Copyright 1949, 1954 by the McGraw-Hill Book Company, Inc. Printed in the United States of America. All rights reserved. This book or parts thereof may not be reproduced in any form without written permission of the publisher.
Library of Congress Catalog Card Number: 58-59655
Published by Whittlesey House,
a division of the McGraw-Hill Book Company, Inc.

Fourth printing

CONTENTS

18-BENNING
JUV
621.388

62X52934
275

WHAT TELEVISION IS

Television means seeing across space.

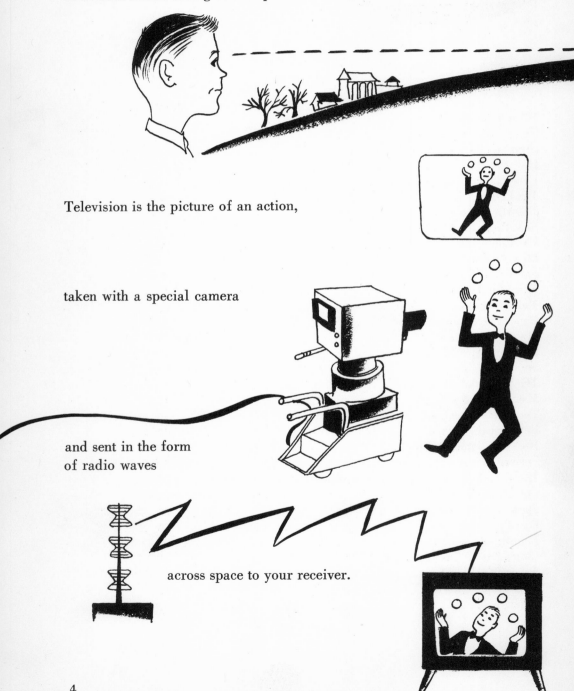

Television is the picture of an action,

taken with a special camera

and sent in the form
of radio waves

across space to your receiver.

Television is an action,
then a picture,
then electricity,
then radio waves,
then electricity again—
and finally a picture again
in your receiver,
all in an instant.

But television is more than this. Television is the greatest mass-communications medium ever invented. This means that more people can both see and hear the sights, sounds, and ideas of the world they live in than ever before.

THE WORDS IN THIS BOOK
(AND SOME OTHERS TOO)

ACTUALITY BROADCAST. Live television reporting of an actual event taking place.

A D. Short for associate, or assistant, director.

AMPLITUDE MODULATION (AM). A way of mixing the signal from the television camera or the microphone with the radio wave that is going to carry it through the air. The waves that carry television pictures are always amplitude-modulated, which means that the size or amplitude of the wave varies.

ANTENNA. The part of the television receiver that picks television waves out of the air, or the part of the transmitter that sends them into the air.

AUDIO. Anything to do with television sound.

AUDIO-FREQUENCY WAVES. Electrical waves of the same length as sound waves.

AUDIO SIGNAL. Sound that has been changed into electrical impulses.

BAND. A range of radio frequencies within two definite limits.

BAT-WING ANTENNA. A television broadcasting antenna made of a series of radiators placed along a mast.

BOOM. A telescoping pole from which the mike is hung.

MIKE BOOM

BOUNCE. Sudden changes in the brightness of the picture.

BRIGHTNESS CONTROL. The knob on your receiver with which you can change the amount of light in the picture.

BUSY PICTURE. One with so much background detail that it is confusing.

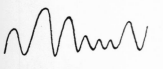

AMPLITUDE
MODULATION

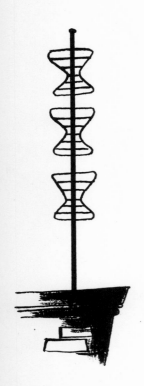

BAT-WING
ANTENNA

CARRIER WAVE. The electromagnetic wave that carries radio or television signals through the air.

CATHODE-RAY TUBE. An electron tube in which the electrons are freed from their source in a ray or beam. The picture tube in your receiver is a cathode-ray tube.

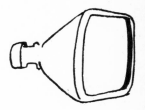

CATHODE-RAY
TUBE

CHANNEL. A band of frequencies given by the Federal Communications Commission to each television and radio station for broadcasting. Within the studio, the sets of cables and monitors assigned to "live," film, and still pictures are called channels.

CLOSED CIRCUIT. Television which is not broadcast for general viewing but is sent directly to selected receivers by means of coaxial cable or relay.

COAXIAL CABLE (COAX). A special copper cable with a conducting wire suspended inside. Also a bunch of these cables bound together.

SINGLE
COAXIAL

COAXIAL
CABLE

COMPATIBLE COLOR. A system of color television broadcasting that can also be picked up as a black-and-white picture by black-and-white receivers.

CONTRAST CONTROL. The receiver knob which regulates the light and shadow of the picture.

CONTROL ROOM. Room where directors and engineers, working with monitors and controls, put a television show on the air.

DEAD SPOT. A place where radio or television signals are received badly or not at all.

DECIBEL. The unit for measuring the loudness of sound.

DIPOLE ANTENNA. An antenna split in the middle.

DIRECTIONAL ANTENNA. Any antenna, either broadcasting or receiving, which sends or receives radio waves stronger in some directions than in others.

DOLLY. A wheeled platform on which the camera is mounted.

DOLLY

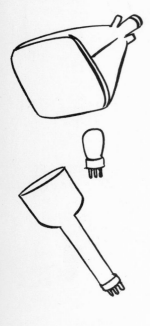

DRY RUN. A rehearsal without studio facilities.

ELECTRON. A minute particle of electricity with a negative charge.

ELECTRON GUN. The place in an electron tube from which a beam of electrons is shot.

ELECTRON TUBE. A vacuum or gas-filled tube where electrons are put to work.

FACILITIES. Cameras, lights, and sound.

FADING. Unwanted lessening and increasing of a radio signal.

FEED. Any picture, sound, or signal received by the studio.

FLUORESCENT SCREEN. A chemically coated screen which gives off light when it is hit by electrons. The receiver screen is fluorescent.

FOCUS CONTROL. The adjustment on the receiver which makes the picture sharp.

FOLDED DIPOLE. A dipole antenna folded back on itself.

FRAME. A single television picture. You see 30 frames a second. When the cameraman "frames" his picture, he gets his subject in just the right place on his camera screen.

FREQUENCY. The number of cycles (or complete motions) of electromagnetic waves in one second.

FREQUENCY MODULATION (FM). A way of varying the frequency of the carrier wave to match the signal. All television sound is FM.

FREQUENCY MODULATION

HIGH-FREQUENCY WAVES. Very short radio waves.

HORIZONTAL HOLD. The receiver knob used to adjust the picture when it slips off to either side.

IMAGE ORTHICON (ORTH). The camera tube. An extremely sensitive electronic tube which needs very little light.

IMAGE ORTHICON

INTERFERENCE.   Any signal, natural or man-made, which disturbs the good reception of the sound or picture.

KILOCYCLE.   A frequency of 1,000 cycles a second.

KINESCOPE.   Film recording of a program, photographed directly from a receiver tube. Also called KINIE.

LEAD-IN.   The wire which conducts the signal from the antenna to the receiver.

LINE.   A single sweep of the electron beam from left to right across the television screen in either the camera or the receiver. There are 525 lines in the U. S. picture. Other countries have different numbers of lines.

LINE-OF-SIGHT.   A straight path from transmitting to receiving antenna, with nothing in the way.

LINE

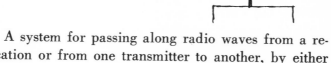

LINE-OF-SIGHT

LINK.   A system for passing along radio waves from a remote location or from one transmitter to another, by either microwave relay or coaxial cable.

LIVE.   Short for "alive"; television of real things and people in action, not film, tape, or still pictures.

MEGACYCLE.   1,000,000 cycles.

MICROPHONE (MIKE).   A device which changes sound into electrical impulses.

MICROWAVE RELAY REFLECTOR.   A dishlike metal reflector behind the antenna or wave guide of a transmitter to focus the microwave signals in one direction.

MICROWAVE RELAY STATION.   A station which automatically picks up and rebroadcasts electromagnetic waves, greatly increasing the distance covered by the original transmitter.

MICROWAVES.   Radio waves less than 1 meter (39 inches) long.

NETWORK.   A group of television stations, connected by coaxials or relay stations, or with a central plan of programming.

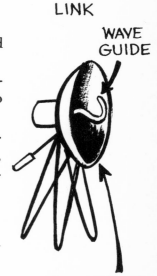

LINK

WAVE
GUIDE

REFLECTOR

NOISE. A spot of unwanted light in a television picture. A noisy picture is one with flashes of light all over it.

ORTHICON. An Image Orthicon or Studio Orthicon camera tube.

PATCH BOARD. A kind of switchboard for connecting studio lights to a light man's control board.

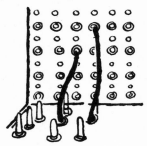

PATCH BOARD

PAY TELEVISION. A system of paying for special television programs, aside from the ones you receive free.

POTS. The volume-control knobs on the audio engineer's desk.

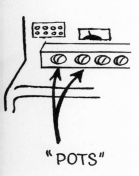

"POTS"

PROJECTION TELEVISION. A combination of lenses and/or reflectors which enlarge a television picture and project it onto a screen.

RACKS. Metal cabinets filled with operating electronic equipment.

RADIATOR. The part of the broadcasting antenna which radiates the waves out into space.

RADIO LINK. See LINK.

RADIO WAVE. An electromagnetic wave made by quick changes of current in the broadcasting antenna, and traveling through space at 186,000 miles a second.

REMOTE. Any program originating outside the studio.

RUN-THROUGH. A rehearsal.

SCANNING. The line-by-line sweep of the electron beam across the screen in the camera and receiver tubes.

SERVICE AREA. The region around a transmitter where its signals can be clearly received.

SERVICE
AREA

SIGNAL. The sound or picture after it has been changed into electricity or radio waves.

SUPER-TURNSTILE ANTENNA. See BAT-WING ANTENNA.

SYNCHRONIZATION (SYNC). The process of keeping the electron beams in the camera and receiver doing the same thing at the same time.

TAPE (AUDIO and VIDEO). A clear tape, coated with iron oxide powder, capable of recording sound and pictures in electrical impulses.

TEST PATTERN

T D. Short for technical director.

TELECAST. The broadcast of a television program.

TELEGENIC. Anyone who looks well on television.

TELOP or TELOPTICON. A device for projecting art work or still pictures.

TEST PATTERN. A drawing of lines and circles broadcast by television stations for testing cameras and receivers.

TRANSISTOR. A crystal capable of performing the same job as an electron tube.

TRANSMITTER. The equipment from which the signals are broadcast.

VERTICAL HOLD. The control knob used to adjust the picture when it slips up or down on the television receiver screen.

VIDEO. Means "see" and is used when talking about the television picture. Sometimes television itself is called "video."

VIEWER. Anyone watching television.

WAVE GUIDE. A hollow metal tube which conducts electromagnetic waves.

WAVELENGTH. The distance between two waves, from the top of one to the top of the next.

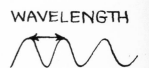

WAVELENGTH

WIDE-ANGLE SHOT. A camera shot taking in a large part of the field of action.

WING IT. To do a show without rehearsal.

ZOOMAR. A lens of variable focal length that can take a close-up or a wide-angle shot from the same position.

ZOOMAR LENS

HOW THE
PICTURE BEGINS

The television picture begins in the camera.
There is no film in a television camera.
Its job is to change the picture it sees into
a sort of electrical picture that can be sent
through wires and across space.

The heart of the camera is an electron tube
called the Orthicon, and it works like this.

1. LIGHT ENTERS LENS

The picture comes in through the camera
lens and is focused on a screen that is sensitive to light. The screen is made of thousands
of tiny, chemically coated spots. As a ray of
light hits each spot, it gives off microscopic
charges of electricity called electrons. The
brighter the ray of light, the more electrons
the spot sends out.

These electrons shoot along to another
screen called the target, hitting it so hard that
they knock more electrons out of the target.
These displaced electrons are collected, leaving the target hungry for electrons.

At the other end of the camera tube is an
electron gun, shooting out a thin stream of
electrons the way a water pistol shoots out
water. This stream of electrons moves swiftly
back and forth across the face of the target,
which has light-sensitive spots too.

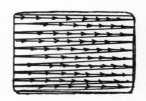

THE BEAM SCANS THE TARGET
SOMETHING LIKE THIS – BUT IT
TAKES 525 LINES TO MAKE A
PICTURE. (THE ONES WITHOUT
ARROWS DON'T COUNT.)

As it moves, each spot grabs electrons back from the stream to replace the ones that were knocked out of it.

Finally the stream bounces back to an electron collection plate. When it leaves the electron gun, the stream is of a constant strength; but when it bounces back from the target it varies, because of the electrons it has lost. The stream varies just as the light and dark varied in the picture that came into the camera lens.

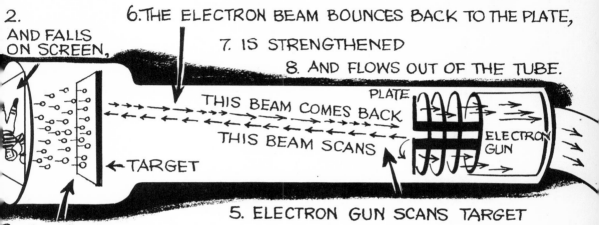

2. AND FALLS ON SCREEN,

6. THE ELECTRON BEAM BOUNCES BACK TO THE PLATE,

7. IS STRENGTHENED

8. AND FLOWS OUT OF THE TUBE.

PLATE

THIS BEAM COMES BACK

THIS BEAM SCANS

←TARGET

ELECTRON GUN

5. ELECTRON GUN SCANS TARGET

3. RELEASING ELECTRONS

4. WHICH FLOW TO TARGET.

The stream sweeps back and forth across the target just the way your eyes do when you read a book. It covers every point in the picture, line by line. This is called scanning.

When the varying beam returns to the plate, it is called the signal, and it is an electrical reproduction of the picture in light that came into the tube. Before it leaves the tube, this signal is made much stronger.

The electron beam scans so swiftly that 30 separate pictures are sent out of the tube every second. This is enough to catch the fastest action going on in front of the camera.

In a studio camera, the tube that does all this work is only about 17 inches long, but it costs about $1,200. The color-camera tube (which we'll talk about on pages 52-53), costs about $1,800. And though the picture on your television screen is much larger, that first picture in the camera tube is $7/8$ inch high and $1\frac{1}{4}$ inches wide.

13

THE TURRET USUALLY HAS A 2-INCH, A 3½-INCH, 5½-INCH AND A 13-INCH LENS FOR SHOTS FROM A WIDE ANGLE TO A CLOSE-UP

SOMETIMES, INSTEAD OF ONE OF THE OTHERS, THERE IS A ZOOMAR LENS

MONITOR

MONITOR

CAMERAS AND LENSES

Usually two or three television cameras are used to pick up a live show. Most cameras have four lenses mounted on a round plate called a turret. Each lens takes a different size picture of the same subject, from a close-up to a long shot. The cameraman gets the lens he wants into position by turning the turret.

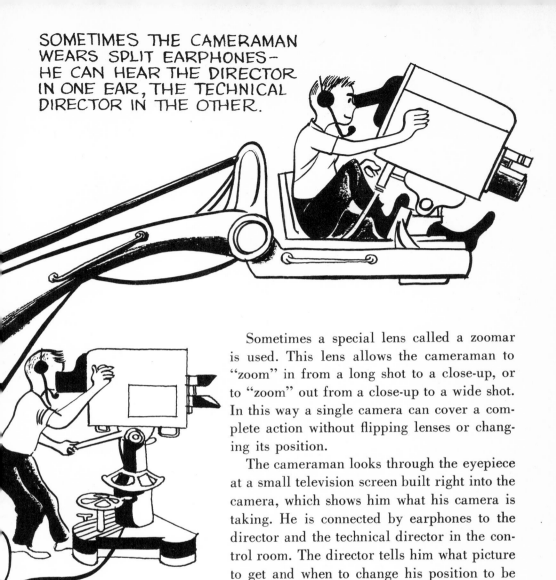

SOMETIMES THE CAMERAMAN
WEARS SPLIT EARPHONES—
HE CAN HEAR THE DIRECTOR
IN ONE EAR, THE TECHNICAL
DIRECTOR IN THE OTHER.

Sometimes a special lens called a zoomar is used. This lens allows the cameraman to "zoom" in from a long shot to a close-up, or to "zoom" out from a close-up to a wide shot. In this way a single camera can cover a complete action without flipping lenses or changing its position.

The cameraman looks through the eyepiece at a small television screen built right into the camera, which shows him what his camera is taking. He is connected by earphones to the director and the technical director in the control room. The director tells him what picture to get and when to change his position to be in place for the next shot.

All studio cameras are mounted on different kinds of wheeled stands. Some are on pedestals that can be pushed, raised, or lowered by the cameraman himself. Other cameras are attached to cranes that are so big it takes two men beside the cameraman to raise, lower, and move them about. Each of these assistants has his own monitor on the crane so that he too can see what the camera is taking.

More compact cameras are built for use outside the studio, and there are even some that can be hand carried. But large or small, all television cameras work alike.

15

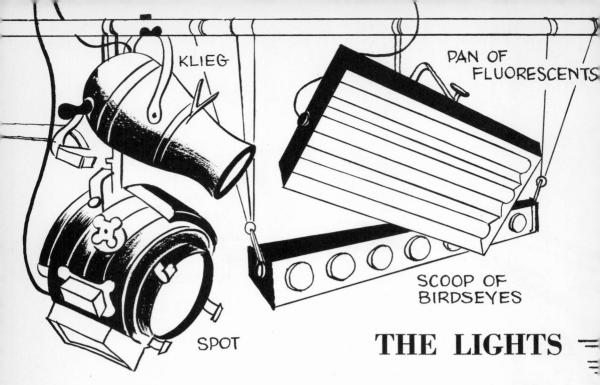

KLIEG

PAN OF FLUORESCENTS

SCOOP OF BIRDSEYES

SPOT

THE LIGHTS

When a television show is on the air, there is little time to adjust the lights. They must be properly placed to light every part of the set.

All the different kinds of lights are hung from pipes that can be raised or lowered from the studio ceiling. Several kinds of basic lighting are used to get good over-all light. One studio may use blocks of 2,000-watt spots. Another may use pans of birdseyes or banks of fluorescent lights. Other, more concentrated lights are used to spotlight the main action and close-ups.

The lighting director works with the director and the set designer and is in charge of lighting the set. During the show he directs his assistants to turn lights on or off, or dim them for special effects. The lights themselves are not moved.

In the biggest studios there is a panel, called a patch board, which looks like a telephone switchboard. The lights are plugged in through this switchboard to a special control panel where the lighting operator sits. Using his lighting script, and listening to the lighting director, he plays the keys of the control panel almost like an organ, turning lights off and on, dimming and brightening them, achieving all kinds of lighting effects.

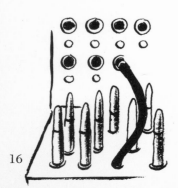

THE PATCHBOARD LOOKS LIKE A TELEPHONE SWITCHBOARD

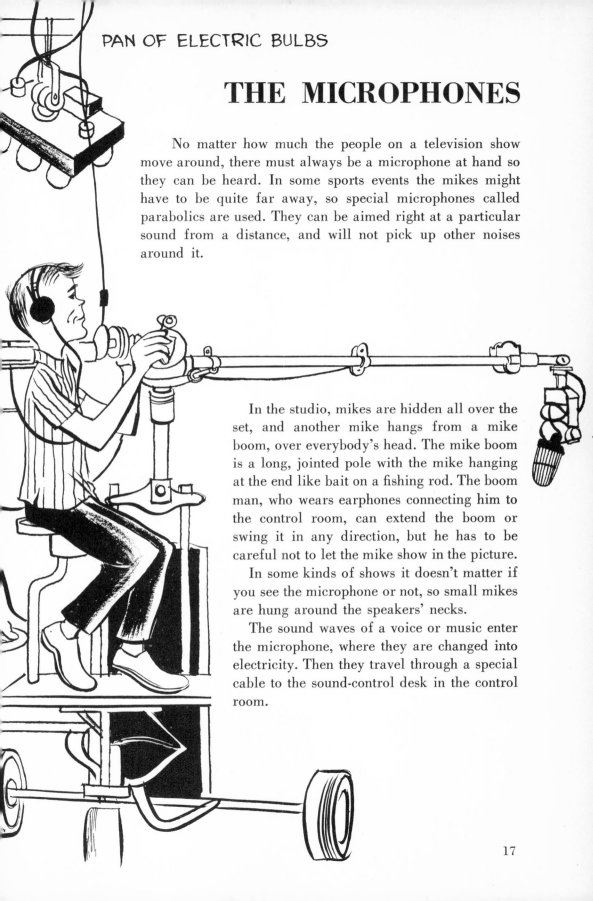

THE MICROPHONES

No matter how much the people on a television show move around, there must always be a microphone at hand so they can be heard. In some sports events the mikes might have to be quite far away, so special microphones called parabolics are used. They can be aimed right at a particular sound from a distance, and will not pick up other noises around it.

In the studio, mikes are hidden all over the set, and another mike hangs from a mike boom, over everybody's head. The mike boom is a long, jointed pole with the mike hanging at the end like bait on a fishing rod. The boom man, who wears earphones connecting him to the control room, can extend the boom or swing it in any direction, but he has to be careful not to let the mike show in the picture.

In some kinds of shows it doesn't matter if you see the microphone or not, so small mikes are hung around the speakers' necks.

The sound waves of a voice or music enter the microphone, where they are changed into electricity. Then they travel through a special cable to the sound-control desk in the control room.

17

SETS, PROPS, AND COSTUMES

When a script is finished, the director, the lighting director, and the set designer get together to plan the set.

The people who design the sets for television shows have to think of some special things. Because the picture on your television set is small, the designer tries to give it a feeling of space. By using perspective cleverly, he makes his sets look deeper from front to back than they really are. He has to be careful not to complicate the background so you can't see the actors clearly.

Sets are built so cameras can look into them from a variety of angles. They peep through doors, picture frames, fireplaces. Sets very seldom have ceilings so that lights can shine right down into them. Cameras on cranes can look down from above too.

After it has been used, scenery is stored in a kind of giant library called the scene dock. In working out the scenery for a new show, as many pieces as possible are taken from the dock, changed if necessary and repainted into a new scene. All sets, even though they are seen in black and white, are painted in color. Most sets are made of wood and masonite so they are strong enough to be used over and over again.

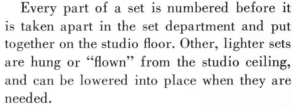

Every part of a set is numbered before it is taken apart in the set department and put together on the studio floor. Other, lighter sets are hung or "flown" from the studio ceiling, and can be lowered into place when they are needed.

When a scene is set up, it is "dressed" with furniture, pictures, ornaments, or other "props," to make it look complete. ("Props" is short for properties.) Most studios have prop departments where ordinary props are kept, but unusual things are rented. A set may need a dozen soda-fountain chairs or a suit of armor or a stuffed moose. It wouldn't be practical to keep all these things on hand, so "prop shoppers" have the job of finding odd things when they are needed.

Costumes are only designed and made to order for very special shows. Otherwise they are rented, then altered to fit the players. The costume department, the set designer, the lighting director, and the director all work together to be sure the costumes photograph well in the sets.

AIR
MONITOR
FOR
AUDIO

AIR OR
LINE
MONITOR

THE CONTROL ROOM

The control room is the center of operations in a television studio. The director and his assistants work here, and so do the video engineers. Some control rooms are placed so that they overlook the action on the studio floor, but most control rooms are "blind," and may be some distance away, even in another part of the building.

The video engineers sit at a control desk in front of a number of monitors, which are television screens. There is a monitor for each camera, which shows what that camera is taking. Other monitors are connected to film or tape channels, slide projectors, even to other studios.

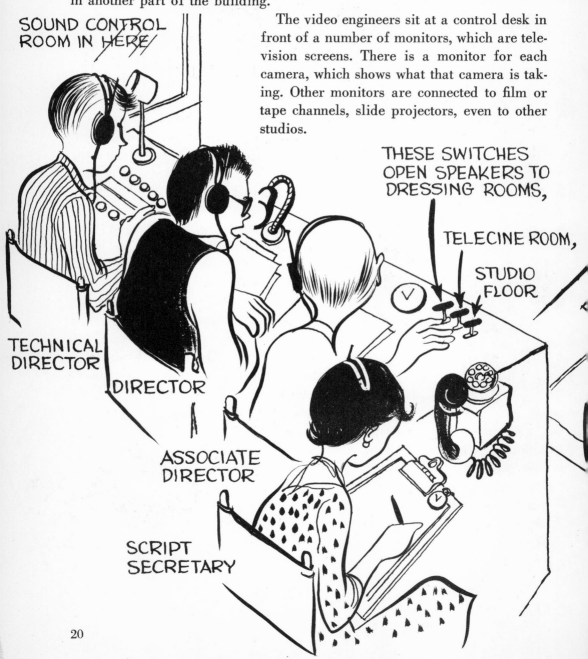

SOUND CONTROL ROOM IN HERE

THESE SWITCHES OPEN SPEAKERS TO DRESSING ROOMS,

TELECINE ROOM,

STUDIO FLOOR

TECHNICAL DIRECTOR

DIRECTOR

ASSOCIATE DIRECTOR

SCRIPT SECRETARY

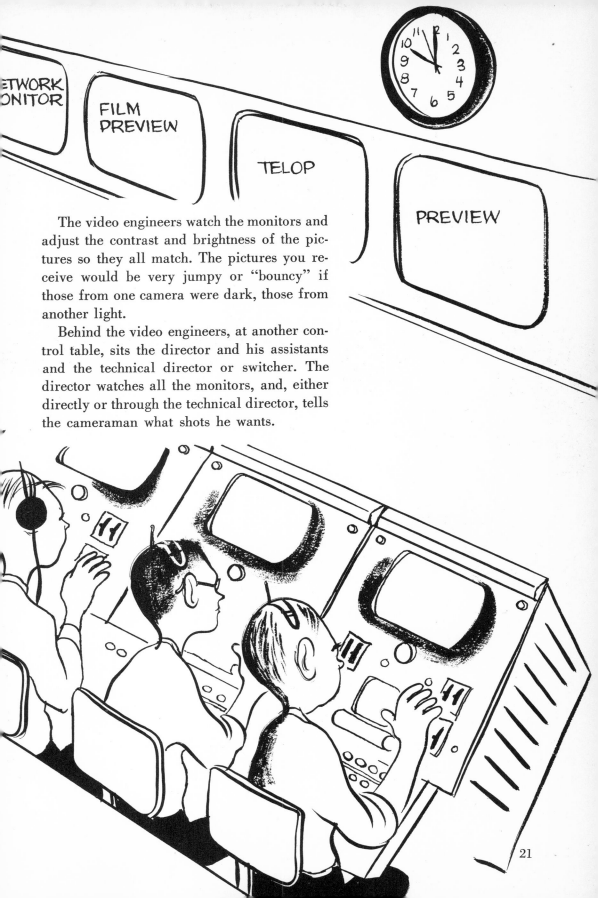

The video engineers watch the monitors and adjust the contrast and brightness of the pictures so they all match. The pictures you receive would be very jumpy or "bouncy" if those from one camera were dark, those from another light.

Behind the video engineers, at another control table, sits the director and his assistants and the technical director or switcher. The director watches all the monitors, and, either directly or through the technical director, tells the cameraman what shots he wants.

During a show all the cameras are operating all the time, and from these the director selects the one to be broadcast. By number he tells the switcher which camera or channel he wants on the air, and the switcher puts it on by pushing the right button. The picture that is being broadcast appears on the air (or line) monitor. Sometimes the cuts come so fast that the switcher or technical director works his control buttons just like a typewriter.

In addition to the monitor controls, the control room has many cabinets or "racks" crammed full of electron tubes. Some supply and regulate power. Others amplify the signal before sending it on. Another set of equipment, called the sync generator, keeps all the camera and film channels, the transmitter, and your home receiver locked together in step.

Because of the heat from hundreds of electronic tubes, control rooms get very hot and have to be heavily air-conditioned.

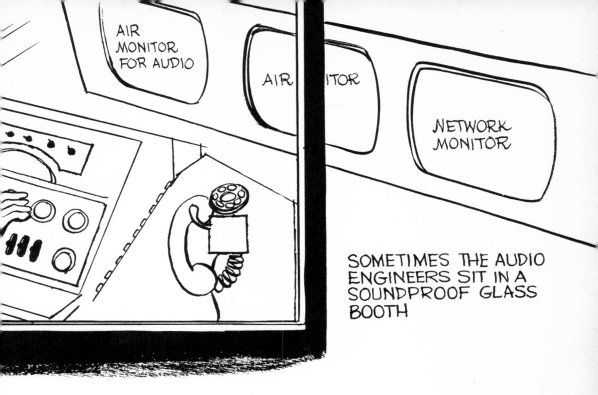

AIR MONITOR FOR AUDIO

AIR [MON]ITOR

NETWORK MONITOR

SOMETIMES THE AUDIO ENGINEERS SIT IN A SOUNDPROOF GLASS BOOTH

CONTROLLING THE SOUND

In a separate part of the control room there is an audio-control board, where the audio engineer works. This board has seven or eight sockets into which microphone cables and other kinds of sound equipment are connected. Each socket is called a position, and there is a knob at each position to control the volume or loudness of the sound. These knobs are called "pots," short for potentiometers. The audio engineer can actually see how loud the sound is on a gadget called the DB (decibel) meter.

During a show, many microphones are used. Some pick up the actors' voices, some the music from the orchestra. The announcer will speak into another, the sound effects man has still others. When sound film or audio tape is being used on the program, this sound is controlled on the audio-control board too.

The audio engineer watches the air monitor to make sure he has the right mikes open at the right time. It is also his job to blend or "mix" all these separate sounds so that you hear them in proper balance.

The audio engineer may also be called on to play records on his two turntables if they are needed on the show. Sometimes there are two engineers to handle all the chores.

LIVE STUDIO SHOWS

When you watch a "live" television show, you are seeing something at the moment it is happening. There is no chance to do a scene over or make corrections, as there is in a show that is done on film or tape. No matter what happens, the show keeps going until it is finished. Whether it is a dramatic show, a quiz, or a musical variety, there is a feeling of something real unfolding.

THE PEOPLE WHO START A SHOW

The program department okays an idea for a show. The producer decides what he wants the show to be like.

The writer puts the idea into words, and the director's job is to make the words into a show. The producer and the director choose the cast with the help of the casting director, decide on the sets with the help of the set designer, select the music with the help of the music director and, if there are dances, work these out with the choreographer.

The program-operations department assigns associate directors and production assistants, studio facilities, and rehearsal time.

The technical department assigns engineering and camera crews.

Network operations notifies other stations in the network of the time of the show and orders the necessary facilities to carry it.

The production department starts work on the costumes, props, and scenery, and the publicity man gets out news stories.

The sponsor's commercials are prepared by the advertising agency.

Dozens of secretaries bang on typewriters, writing scripts and memos.

And the budget department figures out what everything will cost.

REHEARSALS

Some small shows are not rehearsed, but it takes many hours of rehearsal to put on a big studio show. A 90-minute dramatic show takes many days of rehearsal without facilities (which means cameras, lights, and microphones). The actors learn their lines, the sets are put in place, the props are collected.

Then there are several days of rehearsal with facilities. The lights are adjusted and the mikes are set. Camera positions, which have been blueprinted by the director beforehand, are tried out. Facilities rehearsals involve not only the actors, the directors, and the cameramen, but all the technical people on the floor and in the control room.

Then there is at least one more day of complete rehearsal and dress rehearsal to make sure of everything. A big musical variety show takes almost, but not quite, as much rehearsal as a major dramatic show.

ON THE AIR

The sets are in place, the lights are on, the mikes are "hot" (which means open), the actors are in their places on stage, the television cameras are on. The floor manager yells "Stand by!" and awaits further cues from the director and his assistant in the control room over his walkie-talkie.

In the control room the director watches the big clock for the exact second and throws his first cue to the floor manager outside to start the action.

As the director watches the action on the control-room monitors, the assistant director, from his marked script, gives additional directions to the floor manager. The technical director reminds the director of action coming up. The script secretary, or another assistant director, working from a carefully timed script, keeps the director posted on whether or not the show is running exactly on time.

Meanwhile, the director is constantly making cuts from one camera to another and giving directions to the actors through the floor manager. Everyone seems to be talking at once, but there isn't any confusion.

The engineers (who take orders from the technical director) are balancing the technical quality of the pictures, and are pushing buttons to switch cameras. At his control panel, the sound man is opening and closing mikes.

On the floor, the actors are coming and going on cue and watching the floor manager for signals from the director. Sets and props are being swiftly and silently moved into place. Cameras are moving into position to be ready for each planned shot. Cranes are raised and lowered. The lighting director and his people are turning lights off and on.

The hands move around the clock, corrections are made, commercials and station breaks are inserted at the proper times, and the producer is worrying for everybody.

A live show is a tense experience for the people working on it, because even the most careful plans sometime go wrong, and millions of viewers are sitting in on any error. But the people involved are so skillful that errors hardly ever show. When the last fade is made and the show goes off the air, there is a relieved, noisy outburst when the director says, "That's it. Thanks."

SPECIAL EFFECTS—
FOR LIVE TELEVISION
SUPERIMPOSITION

Pictures from two cameras, a camera and a Telopticon, or a camera and film, are sometimes combined to form one picture. A dancer can look as if she were dancing on the clouds by combining a shot of the dancer being taken by the television camera with a film of clouds running through the projector. When you see titles on top of a scene, or people appearing out of nowhere, it is because two pictures are superimposed, which means they are placed one on top of the other.

SPLIT SCREEN

Split screen is a way of sharing the space on your television screen between two or more cameras. Part of the screen shows the picture from one camera, part from another. They are not superimposed. Each picture occupies its own part of your screen.

FILM AND TAPE

Sometimes, on a dramatic show, the director does not want to be confined to the limits of the studio floor, so he will shoot film ahead of time, on location, and cut it into the live performance at the right time. Sometimes he may record some scenes ahead of time on video tape. If an actor plays two parts, for example, and wears different clothes in each part, there might not be time for him to change back and forth as the action moves along. So the television camera will tape him ahead of time playing one character, and he will do the other one live at the time of the broadcast. The tape is cut in and out at the right moments, and you cannot tell the difference.

PROCESS SCREEN

SCREEN

PROJECTOR
BACK HERE

PROCESS
SCREEN

The process screen is a way of projecting motion-picture film from the rear of a translucent screen so that it shines through and forms a background for the action on the set. For example, you may see a boy sitting on a train looking out of the window. The train is an actual set, but the scenery flashing past is on the process screen. Still pictures can be projected as backgrounds too.

COLOR MATTING

Color matting is a way of combining two entirely different pictures so that they appear to be one solid picture. The actor can be set right *into* a scene, not just in front of it as he is when a process screen is used. Nor can you see one picture through the other as you can in superimposition. Color matting is a complicated way of screening out selected parts of a picture that are a particular color, and leaving everything else. Even if it appears in black and white, color matting must be done with color cameras. It is used when actors appear much larger or smaller than their surroundings; when they appear to pass rapidly from one place to another, as from country to country; when people who are actually in different places appear to be together, without a split screen.

LAP DISSOLVES, FADES, WIPES

Transitions from one scene to another are made in several ways. The picture can be slowly darkened by the video engineer until it disappears (fade-out), and the new scene brought up into brightness (fade-in). Sometimes the picture is faded out of the air monitor as a new one is brought in, and they overlap. This is a lap dissolve. Pictures can also be electronically "wiped" off by a new picture. Wipes can be made in many shapes. They might be a circle growing larger and larger, or a wedge moving across the screen.

OTHER EFFECTS

Upside-down pictures are made by using a prism in front of the camera lens.

Whirling pictures are made by revolving a device behind the lens.

Rippled effects are made by having the camera take a reflected image in a rippled mirror.

Distorted pictures (dreams, maybe) are made electronically.

BLUE BACKGROUND

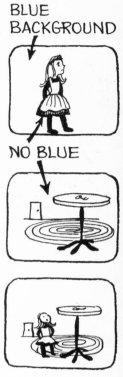

NO BLUE

FILMS FOR TELEVISION

Many of the television programs you see are on film. Some of these films were originally made to be shown in motion-picture theaters, but more and more are produced especially for television.

There are several advantages in telling television stories on film, instead of doing them live.

It is possible to get much more action outdoors than on a set in the studio, with a great variety of locations, far from studio facilities.

Because a film can be made in short "takes," actors have to memorize only a few lines at a time, so less rehearsal is needed.

A film can be made at any time that is convenient for the actors and the director.

Before the show is ever on the air, it has been edited and perfected, and everybody knows it will be just right.

Once a show is on film it can be used over and over again, and it is easy to schedule into many different local program times.

A television "season" is made up, usually, of 39 weeks, so many film programs are done in series of 13, 26, or 39 pictures. Sponsors may buy programs for one third, two thirds, or a full season.

Film series are often syndicated, which means that they are sold to a number of local stations instead of to a network. All of these stations may have different sponsors or several sponsors for the same series.

Because a television series is made up of many stories using the same actors and locations, a whole new technique of film production has been worked out.

Before any shooting starts, a number of scripts are written in the series. Then the best of these is made into a "pilot" film, one complete story in the series which shows the characters, locations, and the kind of stories the series will have. (Often the pilot is made before other scripts are completed.) The pilot is the salesman for the series, and is shown to sponsors and networks until the series is sold. If nobody wants to buy it, the series usually stops right there.

A SINGLE PRINT IN A
SYNDICATED SERIES CAN BE
MAILED TO MANY STATIONS IN
SUCCESSION FOR SHOWING

31

ALL SCENES SHOWING
THE OUTSIDE OF THE
SHIP MIGHT BE SHOT
AT ONCE.

Once the series is put into production, all the scripts are studied and carefully broken down into lists of what sets will be used over and over, what locations will be repeated, what situations will be similar. Then all of these scenes are shot at the same time, even though they belong to different stories. This saves a lot of money, time, and trouble.

For example, if three scripts in a series have Indian battles in them, all the battles would be shot at once, one after another.

If the series uses a ship often, most of the background shots of the ship, for all the stories, could be made at the same time. There are many other ways in which time and money can be saved by working with several stories at once.

There is usually only one producer working on a film series, but there may be several writers and directors working on different stories.

Sometimes the networks make the films themselves, sometimes a star will form his own company to make a series, some films are made by special motion-picture companies that do nothing else, some are made by the major motion-picture companies.

SHOOT
Whale scene- ✓   SCRIPT 1
Storm scene ✓   SCRIPT 3
Becalmed   ✓   SCRIPT 9
Ship with
derelict   SCRIPT 11

A SHOOTING SCRIPT LOOKS LIKE THIS

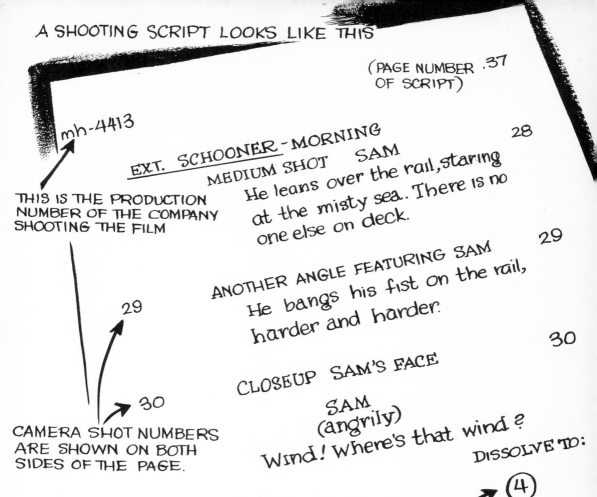

(PAGE NUMBER .37 OF SCRIPT)

mh-4413

THIS IS THE PRODUCTION NUMBER OF THE COMPANY SHOOTING THE FILM

EXT. SCHOONER - MORNING   28
MEDIUM SHOT   SAM
He leans over the rail, staring at the misty sea. There is no one else on deck.

ANOTHER ANGLE FEATURING SAM   29
He bangs his fist on the rail, harder and harder.

29

30

CAMERA SHOT NUMBERS ARE SHOWN ON BOTH SIDES OF THE PAGE.

CLOSEUP SAM'S FACE   30
SAM
(angrily)
Wind! Where's that wind?

DISSOLVE TO:
④

THE NUMBER IN THE LOWER RIGHT- HAND CORNER SHOWS THE NUMBER OF WORDS OF DIALOGUE ON THE PAGE.

The shooting schedule for most stories in a half-hour television series is quite short—about three days. During this time, all the individual scenes of this story are shot. To these are added the necessary background film that has been taken previously, as well as whatever "stock" footage is needed. (Stock footage is film from a film library that has been shot at some other time, maybe years before, for a completely different picture. Some stock shots are used over and over, in many pictures and series; shots of covered-wagon trains, for example.)

All of these parts are edited together, music is added, all the sound is rerecorded, titles and effects are put in, a finished print is made, and the story is "in the can."

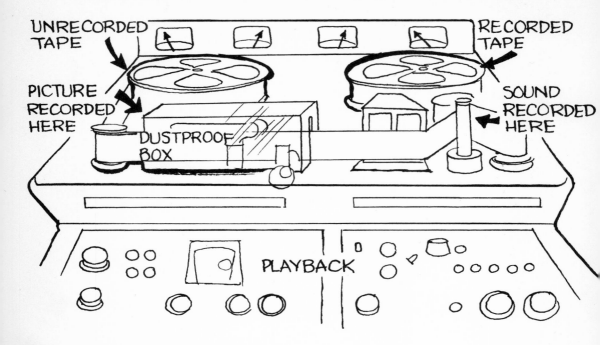

UNRECORDED TAPE

RECORDED TAPE

PICTURE RECORDED HERE

SOUND RECORDED HERE

DUSTPROOF BOX

PLAYBACK

VIDEO TAPE

Video tape is one of the most outstanding advances that has been made in television. It is a way of instantaneously recording, on magnetic tape, the electrical impulses that make up a television picture. Video tape can record anything the television camera can see and the microphone can hear. It does not have to be processed or developed in any way, and can be played back immediately.

The quality of a video-tape recording is so good that it is difficult to tell from a live picture. Not only is its quality better than film, but it is both faster and cheaper. A one-hour program can be recorded on a single reel, while it takes 6 reels to hold an hour of film. The cost of an hour of tape is one quarter that of 16-mm film, or one tenth the cost of 35-mm film.

Video tape has replaced kinescope, the old method of film-recording television programs off the television picture tube.

THE PICTURE AND SOUND ARE RECORDED IN INVISIBLE LINES ON THE TAPE.

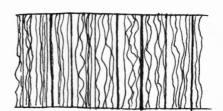

A FRAME TAKES UP ½" ON THE TAPE. TAPE MOVES THROUGH THE RECORDER 15" A SECOND.

Video tape is a clear tape, 2 inches wide, coated with iron oxide, which reacts to electrical impulses. These impulses (the signal from the television camera and the microphone are electrical impulses) form a magnetic pattern on the tape which can be played back into a picture, just as a phonograph record or tape can be played back into music. Once it is recorded, video tape retains its magnetism indefinitely, unless it is intentionally wiped off or erased. Then it can be used again.

A video-tape recorder consists of a console and two racks of electronic tubes. Tape unrolls from the reel past the video head, where four video recorders record on the tape. Then it rolls past the audio head where the sound is recorded. With the addition of two racks of electronic tubes, the same tape and machine can record from a color camera as well as a black-and-white camera.

Video-tape recorders can record programs from studios in the same building or from remote locations coming into the building. They can also record programs that are originating live on one side of the country, to be replayed at a more convenient time on the other.

Video tape is used for:

replaying programs at the same local time in different time belts across the country,

recording live programs for reference or future use,

recording rehearsals for immediate study and correction by the production staff (many live variety and dramatic shows do this),

recording news events which cannot be put on the air immediately,

recording portions of shows which will later be edited together into a complete show,

and for an economical and good-quality syndication of a live-originating show.

A REHEARSAL CAN BE
PLAYED BACK IMMEDIATELY
FOR THE DIRECTOR AND
CAST TO STUDY.

REMOTE OPERATIONS

Any program which does not originate in the studio is a remote operation. Sometimes these programs are staged by the station; for example, a show from a museum or the zoo, or some sidewalk interviews. Sometimes they are public events which are reported by the television cameras, like a political convention or a parade or any sporting event.

When planning any remote show, the director and a survey engineer go out to the location. They check the space they will have to work in, the positions for the cameras, the source of enough electric power to run the equipment, and the location for the relay link, so that it will be in direct line-of-sight with the transmitter. If the program is to be indoors or at night, they have to figure out what lighting will be needed.

After the survey, the director prepares the show pretty much the way the studio director does. If the event is not being produced by the station, his main job is in placing his cameras and mikes so he can get the best possible coverage of the event. He works closely with the people who are putting on the event, so he will know what is going to happen and when.

Hours or even days before the show goes on the air, the engineers move in with over a ton of equipment and start to work. As one group assembles the control-room gear, other engineers string the camera and power cables. Still others set up the microwave relay reflector. (Sometimes the telephone company does this job.)

When remote shows come regularly from the same place, like a sports stadium, the installations there are semipermanent, and all the surveying and setting up does not have to be done each time.

Once the cable is laid, the cameras and lights are set up. The transmitter, the cameras, and the control equipment are all tested, and the intercommunication system among the director, the cameramen, and the engineers is checked. Constant telephone contact is kept with the studio, too.

Now the director takes his place behind the control monitors. If it is a produced show, there are regular rehearsals. Otherwise the crew just runs through camera positions and lenses before the show starts. The director and the cameramen work as a team, following the action with a variety of shots, even though they may never have seen it before.

Sometimes parts of a single show will originate from several locations, perhaps as many as eight or ten widely scattered places, even other countries. In putting on this kind of show, the producer has to consider not only the program material, but coordinating the work of six or seven technical units and six or seven directors in the different locations. He has to see the program from each of the locations, and then rehearse all of them so that they fit together and come out on time. In a program like this, as many as 1,200 people can be involved.

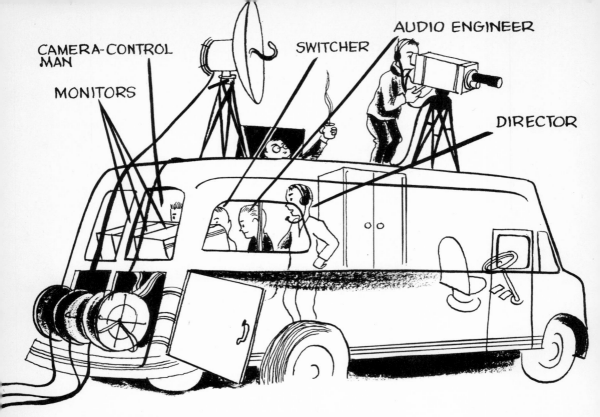

CAMERA-CONTROL MAN

MONITORS

SWITCHER

AUDIO ENGINEER

DIRECTOR

MOBILE TELEVISION

So that you can go places and do things with television, special equipment has been designed to operate on the move. Television cameras can operate from moving trucks, cars, ships, submarines, airplanes, helicopters, and even men's backs.

The most common unit of mobile television is a truck which carries all the necessary equipment, even a control room, wherever it is needed. It is a television studio on wheels.

Not only does the truck carry facilities from one place to another, but all the equipment needed to operate the facilities. At the program location the cameras and mikes are taken out and put where they are needed. Sometimes they are right on the roof of the truck. Sometimes the camera may be connected to the truck by more than 1,000 feet of cable.

These cables connect the cameras and mikes to the control desk in the truck, just as the studio cameras and mikes are connected to the control room. The engineers work in the mobile control room just as they would in the studio. There is usually a video and an audio engineer, a switcher, the director, and maybe an assistant.

Sometimes the mobile unit gets the power to operate its equipment by plugging in to the electric supply of a nearby building. Sometimes it pulls its own generator trailer along.

The mobile truck does not broadcast directly. It sends the signals back to the studio transmitter to be rebroadcast. There are two ways the signal may be sent back to the transmitter. One is through a coaxial cable. But generally the signal is broadcast back to the station transmitter by micro-wave relay.

The microwave relay, which television men call the link, is usually on the roof of the truck. The signal from the relay to the receiving antenna at the station must be in direct line-of-sight. That means there must be nothing between them to interfere. But suppose there are high buildings or moun-tains in the way? Well, then there has to be another link, or two, on a high place that is in line of sight to both the mobile truck and the transmitter, to pass the radio waves along. If the truck is transmitting while it moves, or the tele-cast is being sent from a moving car, one of the engineers has to keep aiming the dish at the receiving point.

When the broadcast is made from a helicopter or an air-plane, the dish is not usually needed. Because of the height of the plane, the signal can be scattered in all directions and still be picked up at the receiving point.

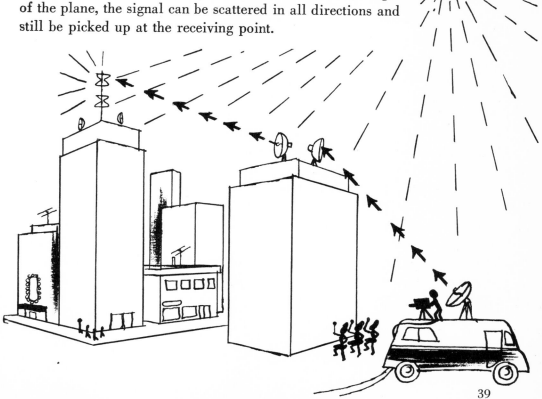

NEWS AND SPECIAL EVENTS

There are several kinds of news shows.

The "news in depth" programs explain and analyze major news happenings. They feature experts in the field, and sometimes the people who are making the news.

Sometimes news is covered live, on the spot. Generally, though, only a spectacular news story is covered this way, because of the time it takes to get mobile equipment to the scene and on the air.

But almost every television station has its own daily, scheduled news broadcasts and, big or small, some kind of news department. The job of all news departments is to get the news on the air promptly and accurately.

In larger stations or networks, getting the program together usually starts with a conference of the news editors and film editor, the director, writers, and commentator, to decide what are the important news stories of the day. The film editor reports what film is coming in locally, from other parts of the country, or abroad. To this film will be added maps and animated charts made in the art department and still pictures from the photographic services that supply the newspapers. The news conference decides the order of the stories and how much time each should take.

Now all departments go to work fast. Film cutters cut and edit the films. Artists draw the maps and charts, writers write the commentary, the picture editor gets the still pictures. By rehearsal time, all the parts of the show are assembled. Sometimes there is live material to be fitted in—perhaps an interview, or direct news pick-ups from other cities. This kind of news show uses all the studio facilities: the news set, the film channel, and the Telop channel. All of this preparation has to be done from the beginning every day. If several news shows are scheduled, much of the material can be repeated.

Special events are often news, but generally can be planned in advance. A political convention, a spectacular parade, a military maneuver, the opening of the opera are all special events.

Sometimes in covering one of these events it is necessary to have remote units at several locations. At a Presidential Inauguration, for example, there would be a unit on the Capitol steps, two or three units along the route of the parade, another might be on the White House lawn, and still another watching the entire scene from an airplane.

The signals from each of these locations are sent to one central control room by coaxial cable or microwave relay link. There is a director with each unit to direct his own crew, and at the central control room an overall director switches from one location to another. From here the pictures are sent to the telephone company for distribution to the stations along the network.

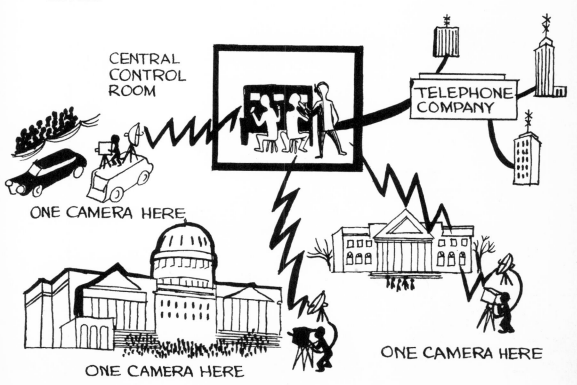

CENTRAL CONTROL ROOM

TELEPHONE COMPANY

ONE CAMERA HERE

ONE CAMERA HERE

ONE CAMERA HERE

THE DIRECTOR
HAS TO CHOOSE

SPORTS

A great number of television hours are devoted to sports. The director who handles television sports has one special problem, and the success of the program depends upon how well he works it out.

Because of the size of the television picture, if the entire field of action is shown (the way you see it when you're there), the individual players are too small to be seen clearly. On the other hand, a close-up of just a few players shuts out the picture of the surrounding action. The director has to compromise between these two choices. He uses a basic shot showing a fair portion of the area, with medium-sized figures. Then he cuts back and forth between close-ups and long shots, giving viewers the impression that they are seeing everything that happens.

Sometimes the commentator who describes the action works in the "cage" with the cameras, sometimes he works in a special press box with other commentators and reporters. But he always has an air monitor right in front of him. While he is talking about the play he sees on the monitor, he has to watch the field too, to see how the complete action is developing. Usually he has helpers who call his attention to things he might not notice and hand him notes about the various players.

Sometimes the technical crews work from the mobile truck, but most major sports stadiums have regular television control rooms. Camera positions are always selected carefully so that the action can be seen from various angles, but without confusing viewers who are accustomed to seeing the entire game from one position.

The cameramen, commentator, and director are a team who must know their sport well, in order to anticipate each play and get the important things on the screen.

Some sports events are very complex and must be covered by a number of units from a number of pick-up points. A major golf tournament is covered this way, as are automobile road races and rowing races. The pictures from each unit are sent to a central control unit, and the director there chooses the coverage from point to point.

Some sporting events, such as a championship prize fight, are not broadcast over the air at all, but are sent closed circuit (we talk about this on pages 58-59) to a special group of theaters and auditoriums which have large-screen television projectors. The audience pays an admission price and watches the event on the large television screen.

Sports telecasts, with their suspense at the outcome, the actuality, the feeling of watching an event at the instant it is happening, is television at its best.

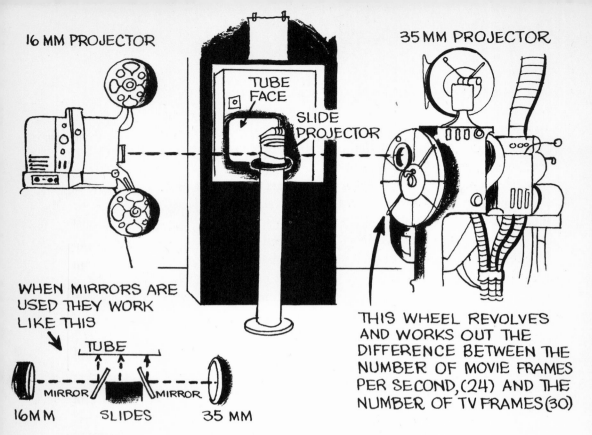

16 MM PROJECTOR

TUBE FACE

SLIDE PROJECTOR

35 MM PROJECTOR

WHEN MIRRORS ARE USED THEY WORK LIKE THIS

TUBE

MIRROR   MIRROR

16MM   SLIDES   35 MM

THIS WHEEL REVOLVES AND WORKS OUT THE DIFFERENCE BETWEEN THE NUMBER OF MOVIE FRAMES PER SECOND, (24) AND THE NUMBER OF TV FRAMES (30)

THE TELECINE ROOM

The room from which movies, slides, and still pictures are sent out over the air is called the telecine room. Some movies are on small-sized film called 16-millimeter (or 16-mm). Some are on larger, 35-millimeter film, which is the kind shown in motion-picture theaters. In the telecine room are projectors for 16-mm and 35-mm film, slide projectors for slides, and another kind of projector called a Telopticon for still pictures or drawings.

These projectors all project onto the face of a special television camera tube. The camera tubes in the telecine room don't have to move around, so they are set in cabinets instead of cameras. But like studio camera tubes, they change pictures into electricity so they can be broadcast.

In some telecine rooms, by using mirrors, several kinds of projectors are arranged to share a single tube.

A number of engineer-projectionists work in the telecine room. Their job is to turn the different projectors on and off on schedule. They put the right films and slides in ahead of time, then get their cues from the director in the control room.

MASTER CONTROL

In a big television station, programs from all studios come from their own control rooms by cable into the master control room, which is lined with cabinets of electron tubes that do all kinds of jobs. Each cabinet has hundreds of wires and connections of its own.

One row of cabinets supplies power to work all the studio equipment —all the cameras, mikes, loudspeakers and control boards. Another row holds the synchronizing equipment, the tubes that keep everything in step.

Many of the cabinets have small screens which look like television screens. But instead of having pictures, the screens show graphs in light of exactly what is happening inside the cabinet. They are called oscilloscopes. Looking at them, the engineers can tell just how that particular rack of equipment is working. They can see trouble in an instant.

The control desk, or console, in master control looks something like the one in the control room. It has many monitors, which show the pictures from different studios and from remote units, the picture on the local television station and the picture on the network (they may be different). There might also be preview pictures from studios about to go on the air, and from the telecine and tape room.

Station-break time is the busiest time in master control. Old programs have to be taken off, new programs switched on, and facilities reassigned.

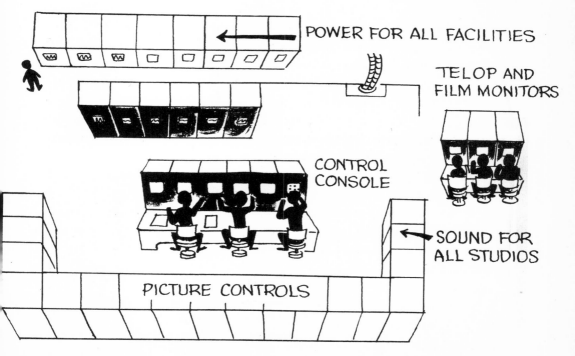

POWER FOR ALL FACILITIES

TELOP AND FILM MONITORS

CONTROL CONSOLE

SOUND FOR ALL STUDIOS

PICTURE CONTROLS

THE TRANSMITTER

The transmitter is usually put in the highest possible place—on top of a mountain or a very tall building. The higher the transmitter antenna is, the greater the area to which it can send programs.

The electrical impulses that are the television signal come up to the transmitter by coaxial cable from the control room or master control. If the program is from a remote unit, it comes directly from that unit by radio relay. The picture and sound signals are always separate.

The transmitter generates the power to carry these signals through the air. The electron tubes that do this work get so hot that they must be constantly cooled by air or water. If the cooling system fails, automatic controls turn the tubes off to keep them from blowing up.

The electromagnetic waves that carry the signal through the air are called the carrier waves. When the signals are added, the carrier has been modulated. The waves that carry the picture are amplitude-modulated, or AM. The waves that carry the sound are frequency modulated, or FM. (More about this on pages 6—8.) The sound and picture waves travel side by side in the channel or band of radio frequencies that is alloted to each station by the Federal Communications Commission.

THE TUBE THAT GENERATES THE FINAL POWER TO BE FED INTO THE ANTENNA IS IN HERE

AM CARRIER STARTS HERE

FM CARRIER STARTS HERE

RELAYING THE SIGNAL

THE VERY SHORT WAVES THAT CARRY THE TV SIGNAL STOP AT THE EARTHS CURVE.

The electromagnetic waves which carry television signals cannot be broadcast over long distances like those which carry an ordinary radio program. Ordinary radio waves take long, easy bounces around the earth. But television waves are very short and they don't bounce. They stop as soon as they come to earth, or go shooting off into space where the earth curves. Direct television broadcasts seldom go farther than 60 or 70 miles.

LONG RADIO WAVES BOUNCE AROUND THE EARTH

A network of microwave relay stations is generally used to send the signal over great distances. These stations are placed on hills or mountains, as far apart as they can be and still be within line-of-sight of each other. On the top are big reflectors which scoop up the television signals aimed at them. Inside the relay station, special equipment strengthens the signals and sends them out again, on to the next station. This equipment works automatically. There doesn't have to be anybody at the station at all.

Coaxial cable is another way of sending television signals. A coaxial cable is a copper tube with a wire suspended inside of it. The inside wire carries the signal, and the tube around it keeps the signal from leaking away.

But a relay signal is more easily controlled and of better quality, so coaxials are generally used over short distances, as from the camera to the control room, and the control room to master control. Then the coaxial links up with the relay.

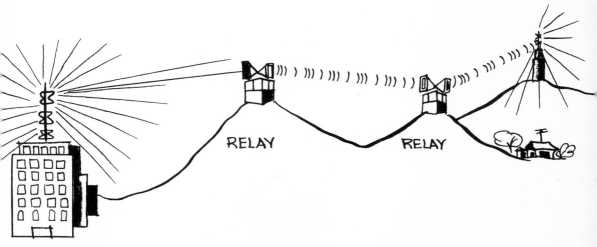

RELAY

RELAY

HOW THE PICTURE IS RECEIVED

When your receiver is turned on, the antenna on your house or on your set picks television signals out of the air. Since every station broadcasts waves of a different frequency, you put your set in tune with any station you want by tuning it in on your channel selector.

The most important part of a receiver is an electron tube, the partner of the one in the camera. This tube is called a cathode-ray tube, and it has an electron gun in it just as the camera tube does.

The big end of the tube is a fluorescent screen. This screen gives off rays of light as long as it is being scanned from behind by the electron gun. The fluorescent screen is your receiver screen, and the rays of light are the television picture.

The beam of electrons in the cathode-ray tube fluctuates just the way the beam in the camera tube does. It shoots out of the gun and scans the fluorescent screen in exactly the same way. Since the beam is made of little charges of electricity exactly like the ones that flowed out of the camera tube, it makes a picture in light on the receiver screen just like the one that first came in through the camera lens. And because electromagnetic waves travel at the speed of light, you see that picture at almost the precise instant the camera sees it. The time it has taken to get to you is too short to count.

The picture on the television screen is really built of 525 lines of light and dark spots, which you can see if you look closely. The beam repeats this 525-line picture 30 times a second. You see all this as a complete and moving picture because your eyes don't work fast enough to see the individual pictures being formed.

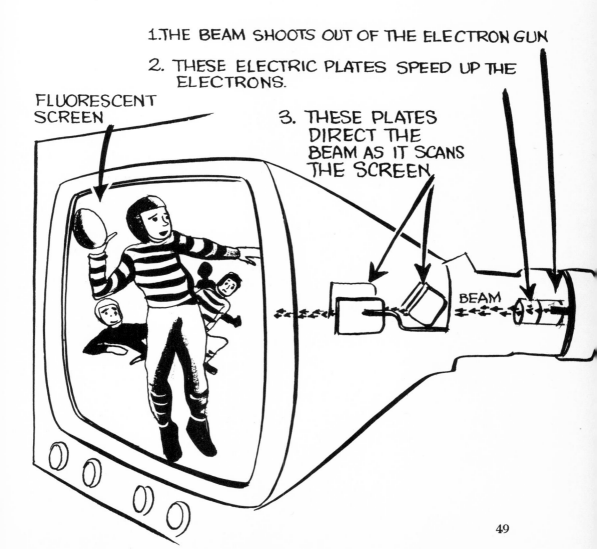

1. THE BEAM SHOOTS OUT OF THE ELECTRON GUN

2. THESE ELECTRIC PLATES SPEED UP THE ELECTRONS.

FLUORESCENT SCREEN

3. THESE PLATES DIRECT THE BEAM AS IT SCANS THE SCREEN.

BEAM

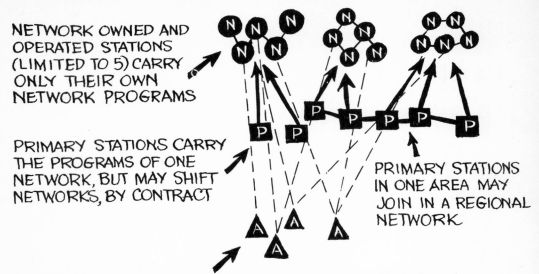

TELEVISION NETWORKS ARE SET UP THIS WAY

NETWORK OWNED AND OPERATED STATIONS (LIMITED TO 5) CARRY ONLY THEIR OWN NETWORK PROGRAMS

PRIMARY STATIONS CARRY THE PROGRAMS OF ONE NETWORK, BUT MAY SHIFT NETWORKS, BY CONTRACT

PRIMARY STATIONS IN ONE AREA MAY JOIN IN A REGIONAL NETWORK

AFFILIATE STATIONS MAY CARRY THE PROGRAMS OF ONE OR SEVERAL NETWORKS, DEPENDING ON THE NUMBER OF STATIONS IN THEIR CITY. (A 1 STATION CITY MIGHT HAVE PROGRAMS FROM ALL NETWORKS ON ITS STATION.)

TELEVISION NETWORKS

A television network is a group of stations which have signed contracts with a key broadcasting company, agreeing to carry all or part of the programs broadcast daily by that company. Up to 5 of the stations may be owned and operated by the key company.

The member stations of a network do not always carry the same programs at the same time, but may broadcast a live show as a video-tape recording at any convenient time. This is important because there is a time difference of several hours in different parts of the country, and a program broadcast at a popular hour in one place might come at an inconvenient time somewhere else.

A network has many advantages. For the public, it offers an opportunity to see the best programs, with talent local stations could not afford. To the sponsor, a network gives an audience of the greatest number of people at the smallest production cost per program. By being able to offer this large audience to the advertisers, the station is able to sell more time. As a public service, a network allows the greatest possible number of viewers to watch important events simultaneously.

THE FEDERAL COMMUNICATIONS COMMISSION

The Federal Communications Commission, or FCC is a government bureau in the Department of Commerce. It regulates and controls the operation of all radio and television stations. It grants licenses to broadcast. (Nobody can broadcast any radio signal without a license, even a "ham" station operator or someone with a telephone in his automobile.) The FCC protects the public interest both in the kind of programs and in the service offered by both radio and television stations.

The FCC also allocates the wavelength that every station must use. Each station has its own channel or band of radio frequencies. Because there are other services that use the frequencies directly above and below the television band, only a limited number of stations can operate in any area without interfering with each other. Stations quite a distance apart can operate on the same channels without any trouble, but to make room for all the stations that want to operate, some are moving into the very high frequency bands.

BECAUSE SO MANY SERVICES USE RADIO WAVES, THE GOVERNMENT ASSIGNS THEM ALL SEPARATE CHANNELS. EACH USER TRANSMITS RADIO WAVES OF DIFFERENT LENGTHS AND FREQUENCIES.

30,000 METERS

↑ VERY LONG WAVES

10 KILOCYCLES

↑ VERY LOW FREQUENCIES

FIXED SERVICES
POINT-TO-POINT
LONG-WAVE
HIGH POWER

COASTAL, MARINE, PRESS ALASKAN, OTHERS

NAVIGATION AIDS
MARITIME BEACONS

COAST·MARINE·SHIPS·MOBILE

STANDARD BROADCASTING

POLICE·AVIATION
RELAY BROADCAST

LORAN

GOV'T·SHIP·POLICE·HARBOR
TELEPHONE·AERO·FORESTRY

HAM

COASTAL·MARINE·OTHERS

HAM

GOV'T·AVIATION·OTHERS

GOV'T·MOBILE·AERO

HAM

COASTAL·MARINE·PRESS
OTHERS

HAM

INTERNATIONAL·SCIENTIFIC
MEDICAL·OTHERS

HAM

NON·GOV'T·FIXED·MOBILE

EDUCATIONAL·FM

FM BROADCASTING

FACSIMILE

GOV'T·AERO,
AIRPORT CONTROL

GOV'T, AMATEUR AVIATION
RADIOSONDE
GLIDE PATH AIDS

CITIZENS RADIO
FACSIMILE

EXPERIMENTAL BROADCAST
NAVIGATION AIDS

HAM

TELEVISION RELAY
METEOROLOGICAL, OTHERS

HAM

GOV'T, FIXED, MOBILE
NAVIGATION AIDS

AIR NAVIGATION, OTHERS

HAM

GOVERNMENT, NON·GOV'T
FIXED AND MOBILE
NAVIGATION AIDS

HAM

NON·GOV'T·FIXED AND
MOBILE, GOVERNMENT

HAM

GOVERNMENT
NON·GOVERNMENT

EXPERIMENTAL

↓ VERY SHORT WAVES

1 CENTIMETER

VERY HIGH FREQUENCIES ↓

30,000 MEGACYCLES

51

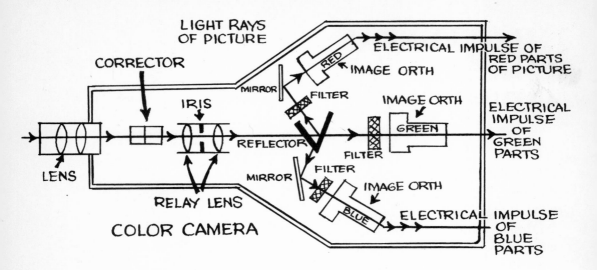

LIGHT RAYS
OF PICTURE

CORRECTOR

ELECTRICAL IMPULSE OF
RED PARTS
OF PICTURE

RED

IMAGE ORTH

MIRROR

FILTER

IRIS

IMAGE ORTH

ELECTRICAL
IMPULSE
OF
GREEN
PARTS

GREEN

REFLECTOR

FILTER

LENS

FILTER

MIRROR

IMAGE ORTH

RELAY LENS

BLUE

ELECTRICAL IMPULSE
OF
BLUE
PARTS

COLOR CAMERA

COLOR TELEVISION

It works like this.

The camera lens focuses the picture through a series of mirrors and lenses onto three separate Image Orthicon tubes inside the camera. The light rays go through a red, a blue, and a green filter, which break the picture up so that the red parts are picked up by one tube, the blue by another, the green by the third. Each tube converts its own color light rays into electrical impulses, which are amplified and transmitted the same way they are in the black-and-white system.

These separate electrical impulses are picked up by the antenna of a color receiver and sent to the tricolor picture tube of the receiver.

This tube has three electron guns in it instead of one. One gun is worked by the electrical impulses from the Orthicon that picked up the red parts of the picture. The second electron gun picks up the impulses from the blue parts of the picture. The third picks up the impulses from the green parts.

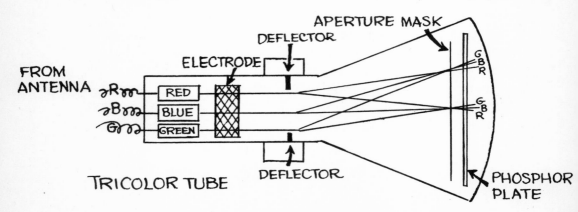

APERTURE MASK

DEFLECTOR

ELECTRODE

FROM
ANTENNA

RED

BLUE

GREEN

TRICOLOR TUBE

DEFLECTOR

PHOSPHOR
PLATE

The three guns shoot their streams of electrons toward a plate at the flat end of the tube. The plate has been carefully coated with an equal number of red-, blue-, and green-colored phosphor dots, arranged in triangles of three each, one red, one blue, one green. There are thousands of these groups of dots in lines across the plate.

Between the electron gun and the phosphor plate is another plate, with lines of tiny holes punched in it. There is a hole for each group of red, blue, and green dots.

The electron streams from the three guns are focused so that they converge at the plate with the holes; and going through every hole the three streams cross.

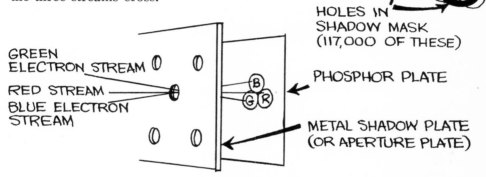

(351,000 OF THESE)
COLOR
PHOSPHOR
DOTS

HOLES IN
SHADOW MASK
(117,000 OF THESE)

GREEN
ELECTRON STREAM

RED STREAM
BLUE ELECTRON
STREAM

PHOSPHOR PLATE

METAL SHADOW PLATE
(OR APERTURE PLATE)

On the other side of the shadow plate, the stream from the red gun hits the red phosphor dot and makes it glow, but the stream is shadowed away from the blue and green dots of that group. The blue and green streams work the same way on their own color dots. Since each electron stream is a translation, in electricity, of the amount of red, blue, or green light that came into the camera tube, it makes its own color dot glow more or less brightly. So in a single group the red dot might be bright, the blue dot just glowing, and the green dot not even activated. This would make that particular group look purple.

The three electron guns scan across every hole, and through it to the phosphors dots, just as the electron gun scans the fluorescent screen in a black-and-white tube. But in the color receiver the picture is made up of thousands of glowing, colored dots. They are so many, and so small, and all this happens so quickly that you see only a clear, steady color picture. You are seeing color television.

AND CAKES MADE WITH THIS FINE FLOUR ARE LIGHTER, BETTER AND

SPONSORS AND COMMERCIALS

Commercial sponsorship pays for most of the television programs that you see. Advertising agencies have found out that television is a good salesman. Because people watch television so closely, they pay more attention to the things they see advertised there, and remember the commercials longer.

There is something special about television commercials that is not true of any other kind of advertising. The product can actually be demonstrated. You can see it and how it works.

Commercials have to be changed often, because people get tired of seeing and hearing the same commercials over and over. They notice repetitions more quickly than they do on the radio or in magazines and newspapers.

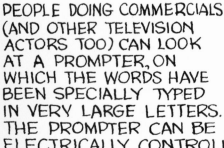

PEOPLE DOING COMMERCIALS (AND OTHER TELEVISION ACTORS TOO) CAN LOOK AT A PROMPTER, ON WHICH THE WORDS HAVE BEEN SPECIALLY TYPED IN VERY LARGE LETTERS. THE PROMPTER CAN BE ELECTRICALLY CONTROLLED SO THAT THE WORDS MOVE THROUGH AT ANY SPEED.

Some film companies do nothing but make television commercials. Writers write special stories. Actors and actresses are hired. Sets are built. Sometimes everybody will travel to another country to get just the right background. Simpler commercials are done live, with perhaps one person giving a salestalk. Many commercials are animated cartoons, and all sorts of new techniques are tried to make them amusing. Commercials are such an important part of most television shows that often they are reviewed by the critics just like the entertainment part of the program.

Television programs not only sell products but create good will for the sponsors. You think well of the sponsor—and the company—that gives you a program you enjoy. The sponsor has to think of all these things, because the cost of putting on a television program is very high. He usually has to pay for the show itself, which may be anywhere from $25,000 to $350,000 for a network show, sometimes even more. He also has to pay the network for the air time he uses on each station, which may add another hundred thousand dollars to his bill.

Sometimes, when the cost is very high, a program will have two sponsors. Each may pay for half of a single show, or they may sponsor it on alternate weeks. Sometimes shows are not sold to any one sponsor, but are paid for by a number of sponsors who buy commercial spots on the show. Sometimes advertisers buy short commercials between shows.

Occasionally a network program will have different sponsors in different parts of the country. Sometimes programs are sold not to sponsors but to single stations in many different places, to schedule and sell as they please. And often a local merchant will sponsor a show that appears only in his own town.

Single stations and networks try hard to find answers to the high cost of putting on a television program.

WAYS OF SPONSORING PROGRAMS

SINGLE SPONSOR
PAYS IT ALL

NETWORK

IF A NETWORK PAYS THE BILL ITSELF, THE PROGRAM IS "SUSTAINING"

SPONSOR
SPONSOR
TWO SPONSORS SHARE THE BILL

SPONSOR
SPONSOR SPONSOR
SPONSOR

MANY SPONSORS BUY SPOT COMMERCIALS

PAY TELEVISION

The television programs you see now are free as the air. You buy your set, twist your dial, and make your choice. The television station or the sponsor pays for the show.

But the cost of putting on a television program is so high that no sponsor or network can afford to pay for some of the programs people would like to see. Pay television is an idea for letting the viewers themselves pay for some special programs. If enough people were willing to pay a "looking price," there would be enough money to bring the opera, ballet, a successful stage play, or perhaps an important new movie into their homes.

So far there are two main ways for putting pay television on your home set.

One is by transmitting it over the air in such a way that the picture is all scrambled up. To make it look right, you would have to put money in a special meter attached to your set or turn a special key which records the fact that you have watched the show. (You would be billed for the program later.)

Another method would bring special programs into your house closed-circuit, through a cable. You would call a central office to be connected into the cable, then charged for the time you watch.

The big question about pay television is how much it will affect free television. Some people think it will simply supply additional hours of good television. Others think it will reduce greatly the number and quality of free programs and services.

EDUCATIONAL TELEVISION

There are almost half a hundred television stations in the United States devoted to education and public service. These stations all operate on a non-profit basis. Some are supported by appropriations from their state governments. Others are connected with universities and are endowed by funds from those universities. Still others are supported by money from foundations.

Educational television stations have two main objectives. One is to further formal education, either in schools or for adults who have not been able to complete their school education but are eager to get their diplomas. The other objective is to give everyone a broader general knowledge of the world, an appreciation of the arts, and the background to become a better citizen.

Some formal courses given over television carry the same kind of credits that regular in-school courses do. The pupils register beforehand, in some cases pay a tuition fee, study, and even take examinations.

Some programs are directed to classrooms in school and are integrated into their regular courses.

Educational television stations bring to many millions of people knowledge of art, science, music, literature. They can see paintings, visit museums, hear music, and discuss books with experts in all these fields, right in their own homes. Sometimes these programs are live, sometimes they are on film. Many universities make a variety of programs to be shown on educational television stations.

Educational television has opened for millions of people a new window on the world.

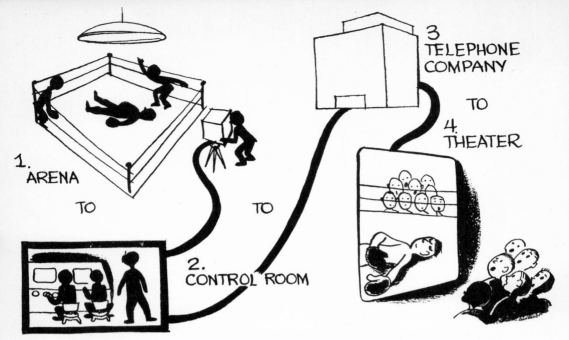

1. ARENA
TO
2. CONTROL ROOM
3. TELEPHONE COMPANY
TO
4. THEATER

CLOSED-CIRCUIT TELEVISION

Closed-circuit television is not broadcast over the air for general viewing. It is sent for a special purpose to a particular viewer or viewers, by means of coaxial cable or relay, directly to the selected receivers. No other sets can tune it in.

There are many uses for closed-circuit television.

One of the most familiar is the broadcast of sporting events into theaters or auditoriums where the audience has to pay to see them. The live cameras are in the sports stadium, and the pictures are sent, by cable or relay, directly to the theaters, either in the same city or across the country. In the theaters they are projected onto a large screen for viewing.

Many experiments have been made in teaching over a closed-circuit television system. A single teacher can give special kinds of lessons to many students in many classrooms, even in many cities, at the same time. Television teaching works out best for lectures, scientific demonstrations, and many kinds of films. It will never be an everyday teacher, because a television set can't answer questions or exchange ideas.

Over closed-circuit television—

A famous surgeon can demonstrate an operation technique to many doctors and medical students across the country.

Radioactive experiments can be observed from a safe distance. The television camera, which is not affected by radiation, can be right in the "hot spot"; the television receiver can be rooms, or even miles, away. Special equipment allows watching scientists to control experiments as they watch.

Military officers, either in battle or maneuvers, can observe action in the field from several vantage points by means of a closed-circuit television camera operating from an observation plane.

Firing and take-off of missiles can be watched closely from a safe distance.

A traffic-control officer at police headquarters, observing traffic movements at critical spots by means of closed-circuit television, can prevent traffic jams by broadcasting announcements, by changing signals, by ordering additional officers to the scene. Some police helicopters have cameras in them to do the same work.

A single security guard can watch many gates of a factory at the same time.

A railroad clerk in a freight-yard office can check the names on freight cars coming into the yard from many directions, then direct individual cars to the proper sidings.

Signatures on checks presented at branch offices of a bank can be identified instantly at the main office.

A new product can be introduced and demonstrated to salesmen at sales meetings in many places.

All kinds of underwater work can be watched and directed from the surface, or even from shore.

Many industrial processes are watched over closed-circuit television (steel, melting in a blast furnace, for example).

Wherever seeing over a distance is helpful, closed-circuit television can be on the job.

ROCKET FIRING

FREIGHT-CAR "HUMPING"

SECURITY CHECK

SIGNATURE IDENTIFICATION

UNDERWATER WORK

AROUND THE WORLD

The people of almost 50 countries have television. In many of these countries, television stations are owned and operated by the governments. In some—Great Britain, Japan, Canada, and others, there are both government and privately owned networks.

No country broadcasts as many hours of television as the United States does. Some stations abroad are only on the air an hour a week.

Programming in most of these countries is different too. Many countries feel that television has given them a unique opportunity to educate their people and to broaden both their knowledge of their own country and of the outside world. Most programs are cultural and educational, with a good deal of music and ballet. Dramatic presentations are generally of great plays. Actuality broadcasts and sports are a very popular kind of television abroad.

Many countries are close to one another geographically, but cannot receive each others' broadcasts because their systems are different. The television pictures of some countries are made up of 525 lines, some of 405 lines, some 625 lines, and some 819 lines. Television receivers that are set for scanning one number of lines cannot receive pictures transmitted in another.

In North and South America almost all countries broadcast a 525-line picture, which is why you can receive programs from Canada, Mexico, Cuba, and the Bahamas. Japan, the Philippines, and Hawaii are on a 525-line standard too.

Most countries in continental Europe broadcast 625 lines. So do Russia and Australia. France and most French-speaking countries in Europe and Africa broadcast and receive 819 lines. Great Britain works on a 405-line system all her own.

Sometimes European countries are interconnected as a network to receive special programs. So that everyone can watch, the picture has to be converted into the standard of each country. A station must receive the program on a receiver that corresponds to the number of lines transmitted. A live television camera, operating on the country's own standard, focuses on that receiver. Then the picture from this camera is transmitted over its own network. This is all done instantaneously, and everyone is seeing the action as it takes place.

There is a considerable exchange of film or recorded programs between countries. Many United States programs are "dubbed" in foreign languages and shown abroad.

Committees are always working to make television standards more universal and to perfect equipment that will handle transmission of different standards. Standards will have to be unified world wide, because sometime soon improved relay methods will be able to carry programs throughout the world instantly.

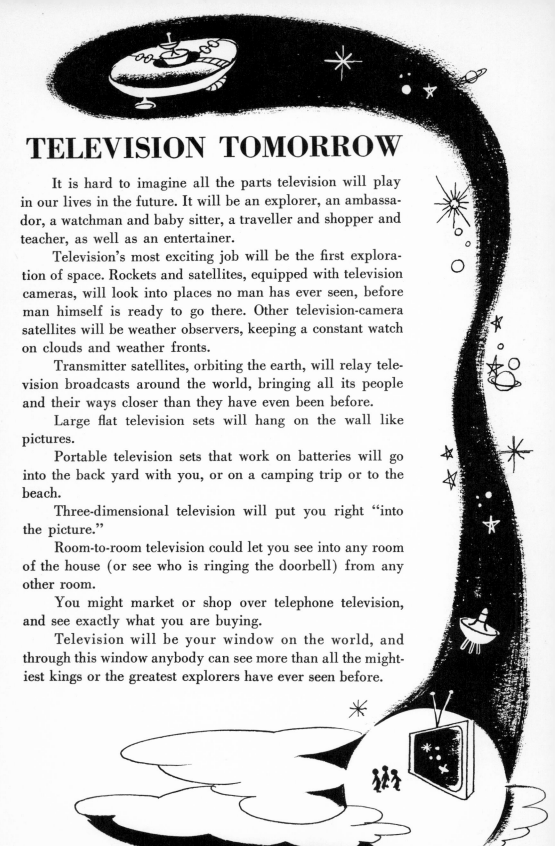

TELEVISION TOMORROW

It is hard to imagine all the parts television will play in our lives in the future. It will be an explorer, an ambassador, a watchman and baby sitter, a traveller and shopper and teacher, as well as an entertainer.

Television's most exciting job will be the first exploration of space. Rockets and satellites, equipped with television cameras, will look into places no man has ever seen, before man himself is ready to go there. Other television-camera satellites will be weather observers, keeping a constant watch on clouds and weather fronts.

Transmitter satellites, orbiting the earth, will relay television broadcasts around the world, bringing all its people and their ways closer than they have even been before.

Large flat television sets will hang on the wall like pictures.

Portable television sets that work on batteries will go into the back yard with you, or on a camping trip or to the beach.

Three-dimensional television will put you right "into the picture."

Room-to-room television could let you see into any room of the house (or see who is ringing the doorbell) from any other room.

You might market or shop over telephone television, and see exactly what you are buying.

Television will be your window on the world, and through this window anybody can see more than all the mightiest kings or the greatest explorers have ever seen before.

INDEX

INDEX